SPOOKY FACTS
FOR BRAVE KIDS

BRIGHT MINDS LEARNING

Bright Minds Learning

Bright Minds Learning

TABLE OF CONTENTS

INTRODUCTION

Are you ready to dive into a world where spooky meets spectacular?

Whether you're a curious cat who loves solving mysteries or a daring adventurer eager to explore the unknown, this book is packed with everything you need to have a frightfully good time! From creepy critters to haunted houses, we've got spine-tingling facts and eerie tales that'll make you wonder what's lurking in the shadows.

But the fun doesn't stop there! This book is loaded with interactive games—think tricky trivia, and clues that will put your detective skills to the test. You can challenge your friends, crack the codes, and uncover the most bizarre and spooky facts together.

So grab your flashlight, gather your courage, and get ready to embark on an adventure that's as fun as it is frightful. Let's see if you're brave enough to unravel the world's mysteries, one spooky fact at a time. Let the Halloween fun begin!

HALLOWEEN
TRICK OR TREAT

CHAPTER 1

THE BEASTS
OF
DARKNESS

When the sun dips below the horizon, the real fun begins. The night is when nature's creepiest, crawliest, and most mysterious creatures come out to play.

These nighttime critters aren't just out for a midnight snack— they're the true masters of the dark, from bats swooping silently overhead to wolves howling under a full moon.

In this chapter, we're diving into the world of nocturnal beasts, where every rustle and hoot could be something with fangs—or just your cat knocking over the Halloween candy.

Ready to get your fright on?

ECHOES IN THE NIGHT

1 **MEDIEVAL FOLKLORE BELIEVED THAT IF A BAT FLEW AROUND YOUR HOUSE ON HALLOWEEN NIGHT, IT WAS A SIGN THAT GHOSTS WERE NEAR.**

Spooky, right? But this is just a myth. Bats are more active at night, using their amazing echolocation to hunt for insects.

2 **THERE ARE OVER 1,400 SPECIES OF BATS, MAKING UP ABOUT 20% OF ALL MAMMAL SPECIES.**

They are found on every continent except Antarctica.

3 **MEET THE BUMBLEBEE BAT, THE TINIEST BAT AROUND, WEIGHING LESS THAN A PENNY WITH A WINGSPAN OF ABOUT 6 INCHES.**

On the other end of the spectrum, the flying fox (or fruit bat) boasts an impressive wingspan of up to 6 feet!

BATS ARE NATURE'S PEST CONTROLLERS.

Some species can gobble up to 1,200 mosquitoes in just an hour, which is great news for anyone who dislikes those pesky bugs.

THERE IS A BAT SPECIES CALLED VAMPIRE BAT.

Found in Central and South America, these nocturnal creatures feed on the blood of livestock. They make a tiny cut with their teeth and then lap up the blood with their tongues. Creepy yet fascinating! Even more amazing, their saliva contains a protein that has been found to help stroke patients.

BATS ARE THE ONLY MAMMALS CAPABLE OF SUSTAINED FLIGHT.

Their wings are made up of elongated fingers covered by a thin membrane of skin.

MANY BATS "SEE" WITH SOUND BY EMITTING HIGH-PITCHED NOISES THAT BOUNCE OFF OBJECTS.

This process, known as echolocation, helps them navigate and hunt in the dark.

IN SOME CULTURES, BATS ARE SYMBOLS OF GOOD LUCK AND PROSPERITY.

In China, they're associated with happiness and long life.

9

BATS PLAY A VITAL ROLE IN POLLINATION AND SEED DISPERSAL.

Species like the lesser long-nosed bat help pollinate plants like agave, which is used to make tequila.

10

LESS THAN 1% OF BATS CARRY RABIES.

They are generally not aggressive and prefer to avoid humans.

11

AND LET'S NOT FORGET THE GHOST BAT, WITH ITS WHITE FUR MAKING IT LOOK LIKE A LITTLE FLYING GHOST OF THE NIGHT!

WHISKERED PHANTOMS

1 A HOUSE CAT IS MORE LIKE A MINI TIGER.

Its genome is 95.6 percent tiger, and they share many behaviors with their jungle ancestors.

 2 CATS CANNOT TASTE SWEETNESS.

 3 CATS' COLLARBONES DON'T CONNECT TO THEIR OTHER BONES.

Instead, these bones are buried in their shoulder muscles, allowing for a greater range of motion and agility.

4 CATS HAVE AN EXTRA ORGAN THAT ALLOWS THEM TO TASTE SCENTS IN THE AIR.

This is why your cat stares at you with her mouth open from time to time. It's called the Jacobson's organ, and it adds to their mysterious allure.

 5 CATS ARE EFFICIENT EATERS WITH ROUGH TONGUES THAT CAN LICK A BONE CLEAN OF ANY SHRED OF MEAT.

Their tongues are covered in tiny, hook-like structures called papillae, perfect for scraping off every last bit.

 6 CATS, CAMELS AND GIRAFFES HAVE SOMETHING IN COMMON.

They walk the same, moving both their right feet first, then both left feet. No other animals walk this way.

7

CATS ARE METICULOUS ABOUT THEIR HYGIENE AND SPEND UP TO A THIRD OF THEIR WAKING HOURS TO GROOM.

This ritual keeps their fur clean and helps regulate their body temperature.

8

CATS ARE LACTOSE INTOLERANT.

While many people assume that cats love milk, the truth is that most cats are unable to digest lactose, the main sugar found in milk.

9

BLACK CAT SYNDROME

Black cats are less likely to be adopted than cats of other colors, a phenomenon known as "black cat syndrome."

10

THE BLACK BOMBAY CAT BREED WAS SPECIFICALLY DEVELOPED TO RESEMBLE A MINI BLACK PANTHER.

11

THE SYMBOL OF A GODDESS: BLACK CATS

In ancient Egypt, around 950 BCE, black cats were revered and considered symbols of Bastet, the goddess of home and fertility. Egyptians believed these cats brought protection and good fortune. Harm to a black cat was severely punished, reflecting their sacred status in society.

BLACK FUR CAN HELP CATS STAY COOLER IN HOT CLIMATES BY ABSORBING AND DISSIPATING HEAT MORE EFFICIENTLY.

 BLACK CATS HAVE A HIGHER RESISTANCE TO MANY DISEASES DUE TO GENETIC MUTATIONS.

 IN THE US AND MUCH OF EUROPE, CROSSING PATHS WITH A BLACK CAT IS CONSIDERED BAD LUCK.

But in the UK, it's believed to bring prosperity and good fortune.

 NATIONAL BLACK CAT DAY

October 27th is celebrated as National Black Cat Day to promote adoption and debunk myths surrounding black cats.

 OSCAR THE CAT

A pet cat named Oscar resided in a nursing home and was believed to be able to tell when one of the residents would soon die. He'd sleep beside them until they passed.

WEBS OF TERROR

1 THE LARGEST SPIDER IN THE WORLD

The Goliath birdeater holds the title of the largest spider in the world, boasting a leg span of up to 11 inches and weighing as much as 6 ounces. Imagine encountering that on a dark night!

2 SPIDER SILK IS FIVE TIMES STRONGER THAN STEEL OF THE SAME DIAMETER.

A single strand can catch a flying insect in mid-air.

3 THE BLACK WIDOW'S VENOM

The black widow spider is infamous for the female's red hourglass marking and venom, which is 15 times stronger than a rattlesnake's. Handle with care!

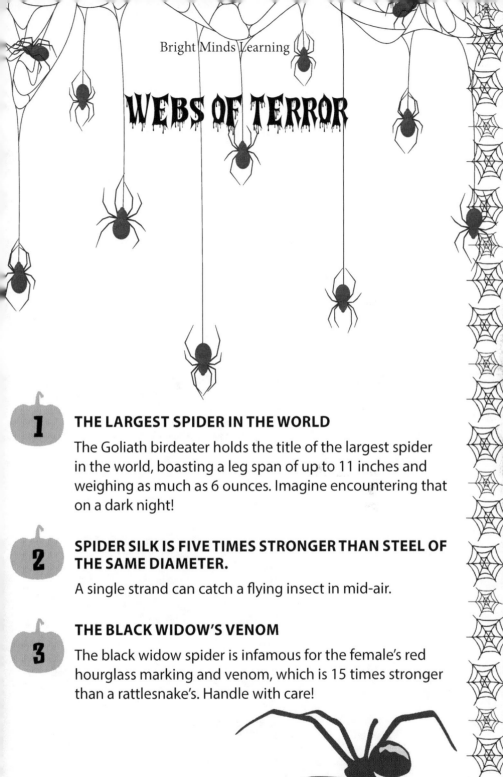

 4 SPIDERS USE HYDRAULIC PRESSURE TO EXTEND THEIR LEGS, PUMPING FLUID INTO THEM TO MOVE.

Unlike most creatures, they lack extensor muscles, making their movement unique.

 5 SPIDER LIFESPAN

The average house spider can live for about one to two years, but some species, like tarantulas, can live for over 20 years in captivity. That's a long time to weave webs and catch prey.

 6 JUMPING SPIDERS ARE THE ACROBATS OF THE SPIDER WORLD, WITH EXCEPTIONAL VISION AND THE ABILITY TO LEAP UP TO 50 TIMES THEIR BODY LENGTH.

They use this impressive skill to pounce on unsuspecting prey.

 7 TARANTULAS CAN REGENERATE LOST LEGS DURING MOLTING.

This process can occur several times throughout their lives, ensuring they stay agile and ready for action.

 8 ORB-WEAVER SPIDERS BUILD NEW WEBS EVERY DAY.

They have tiny hairs called setae on their legs, which detect vibrations.

 9 SPIDERS HAVE CLEAR BLOOD.

 10 CLIMATE CHANGE IS MAKING SPIDERS BIGGER, AND INCREDIBLY, SPIDERS CAN EVEN SURVIVE IN SPACE!

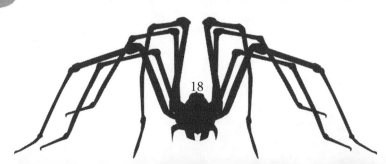

11 SOME FEMALE SPIDERS ALLOW THEIR YOUNG TO EAT THEM ALIVE.

12 THE RED WIDOW MALE FORCE-FEEDS HIMSELF TO THE FEMALE BY PLACING HIMSELF INTO HER MANDIBLES.

If she spits him out, he keeps putting himself there until she eventually eats him. Love can be deadly in the spider world!

13 THERE ARE OVER 100 SPECIES OF SPIDERS THAT MIMIC ANTS, HAVING EVOLVED SIMILAR APPEARANCES AND EVEN SIMILAR PHEROMONES.

Most do this to evade predators, but a few use this disguise to prey on ants.

14 SOME SPIDERS EAT THEIR OWN WEBS, RECYCLING THE SILK TO USE AGAIN.

It's a sustainable way to keep building their homes.

15 SPIDERS CAN'T EAT SOLID FOOD.

They inject venom through hollow fangs to kill their prey, with enzymes that start to liquefy the food. You'll never look at juice boxes the same way again!

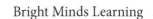

NIGHTTIME WATCHERS

1. OWLS CAN ROTATE THEIR HEADS UP TO 270 DEGREES, ALLOWING THEM TO SEE IN ALMOST ALL DIRECTIONS WITHOUT MOVING THEIR BODIES.

This uncanny ability makes them seem almost otherworldly.

2. THE SILENT FLIGHT OF AN OWL

With specialized feathers that allow them to fly silently, owls are the stealthy ninjas of the bird world. Their silent flight aids them in sneaking up on unsuspecting prey.

3. THE BARN OWL'S HEART-SHAPED FACE HELPS FUNNEL SOUND TO ITS EARS, GIVING IT EXCEPTIONAL HEARING.

This makes them excellent hunters, even in complete darkness.

4. OWLS ARE NOCTURNAL.

Which means they are most active at night, which adds to their mysterious reputation.

5. WHY DO WE SAY OWLS ARE WISE?

In ancient Greek mythology, owls are associated with Athena, the goddess of wisdom, and are considered symbols of knowledge.

6. SOME OWL SPECIES, LIKE THE SNOWY OWL, ADAPT TO HARSH, COLD ENVIRONMENTS AND HAVE THICK FEATHERS FOR INSULATION.

These adaptations help them survive and thrive in extreme conditions.

7 OWLS SWALLOW THEIR PREY WHOLE.

After that, they regurgitate indigestible parts like bones and fur in pellets.

8 OWLS' LARGE, TUBE-SHAPED EYES ARE COMPLETELY IMMOBILE.

This provides a binocular vision that fully focuses on their prey and boosts depth perception.

9 SOME OWLS HUNT OTHER OWLS.

Great horned owls are the top predators of the smaller barred owls.

10 THERE ARE OVER 200 SPECIES OF OWLS.

The tiniest owl in the world is the elf owl, which is 5 to 6 inches tall and weighs about 1 ½ ounces. In contrast, the largest North American owl, in appearance, is the great gray owl, which can grow up to 32 inches tall.

11 THE NORTHERN HAWK OWL CAN DETECT A VOLE FROM UP TO HALF A MILE AWAY, PRIMARILY BY SIGHT.

12 IN A SPOOKY TWIST OF NATURE, OWLS OFTEN FEED THE STRONGEST BABIES FIRST.

This ensures that the most viable offspring survive, but it's a harsh reality for the weaker chicks.

HOPPING HORRORS

1 ONE GRAM OF THE TOXIN PRODUCED BY THE SKIN OF THE GOLDEN POISON DART FROG COULD KILL 100,000 PEOPLE.

It's like nature's own deadly potion, bottled up in a tiny, colorful package.

2 TOADS CAN LIVE FOR A SURPRISINGLY LONG TIME.

Some species, like the American toad (Anaxyrus americanus), can live up to 30 years in captivity. The common European toad (Bufo bufo) can live up to 40 years.

3 TOADS HAVE PAROTOID GLANDS BEHIND THEIR EYES THAT RELEASE A CONCENTRATED TOXIN CALLED BUFOTOXIN WHEN THREATENED.

Unlike the general skin toxins, bufotoxin is secreted specifically during direct threats, making it more effective for defense.

4 THE NATTERJACK TOAD IS KNOWN FOR ITS LOUD AND PERSISTENT NIGHTTIME CALLS, OFTEN HEARD IN EUROPEAN MARSHLANDS.

According to Halloween tales, villagers would hear the eerie "ratcheting" calls of the natterjack toad and believe it to be the chanting of witches brewing potions in the marshes.

IN CHINESE CULTURE, A TOAD ENTERING YOUR HOME IS BELIEVED TO BE A SIGN OF GOOD FORTUNE AND WEALTH.

This belief is often linked to the mythical "money toad," or Jin Chan, which is said to bring prosperity and abundance.

 TOADS HIBERNATE DURING THE WINTER IN COLDER CLIMATES, BURROWING INTO MUD OR LEAF LITTER TO STAY WARM.

 WHEN A FROG SWALLOWS FOOD, IT PULLS ITS EYES DOWN INTO THE ROOF OF ITS MOUTH TO HELP PUSH THE FOOD DOWN ITS THROAT.

This quirky eating habit makes them look like something out of a horror movie.

 THE WORLD'S LARGEST FROG IS THE GOLIATH FROG OF WEST AFRICA.

It can grow to 15 inches and weigh up to 7 pounds. That's the weight of a newborn baby! Imagine that giant hopping around in the night.

 LAUNCHED BY THEIR LONG LEGS, MANY FROGS CAN LEAP MORE THAN 20 TIMES THEIR BODY LENGTH.

They might just leap right out of your nightmares!

 THE COSTA RICAN FLYING TREE FROG SOARS FROM BRANCH TO BRANCH WITH THE HELP OF ITS FEET.

Picture this flying creature gliding through the moonlit jungle.

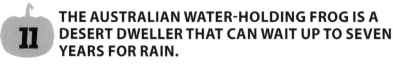

11 **THE AUSTRALIAN WATER-HOLDING FROG IS A DESERT DWELLER THAT CAN WAIT UP TO SEVEN YEARS FOR RAIN.**

It burrows underground and surrounds itself in a transparent cocoon made of its own shed skin.

12 **THE GASTRIC BROODING FROGS SWALLOW THEIR FERTILIZED EGGS.**

The tadpoles remain in her stomach for up to eight weeks, finally hopping out of her mouth as little frogs.

13 **GLASS FROGS MAKE THEIR SKIN TRANSPARENT BY HIDING RED BLOOD CELLS IN THEIR LIVERS.**

14 **A FROG COMPLETELY SHEDS ITS SKIN ABOUT ONCE A WEEK.**

The frog usually eats it after it pulls off the old, dead skin. This weekly ritual is a bit macabre, wouldn't you say?

15 **FROGS CAN STILL DROWN.**

If their lungs fill with water or there's not enough oxygen in the water they're swimming in, these amphibious creatures can meet a grim fate.

HOWLERS IN THE MOONLIGHT

1 **WOLVES CAN TRAVEL UP TO 30 MILES IN A SINGLE DAY WHILE HUNTING FOR FOOD.**

Imagine them stealthily moving through the dark forest, eyes glinting with determination.

2 **THE GRAY WOLF IS THE LARGEST MEMBER OF THE CANINE FAMILY, WITH MALES WEIGHING UP TO 175 POUNDS.**

These formidable beasts are true giants of the night, creeping silently under the cover of darkness.

3 **WOLVES DON'T HOWL AT THE MOON.**

Howling is their way of communicating with the pack. Each howl is unique and can be heard up to 10 miles away, echoing through the night like a haunting serenade.

4

THE WOLF'S SENSE OF SMELL IS 100 TIMES GREATER THAN A HUMAN'S.

Thanks to as many as 200 million olfactory cells, they can detect prey from over a mile away.

5

ARE WOLVES ENDANGERED?

The red wolf, native to the southeastern United States, is one of the world's most endangered canids, with fewer than 300 individuals remaining.

6

WOLVES TREASURE FAMILY.

Wolves are known for their strong family bonds and often share food with their pack members. They care for injured or sick pack members.

7

WHEN IT COMES TO FEASTING, WOLVES CAN EAT A HUGE AMOUNT—AS MUCH AS 9 KG IN ONE SITTING!

Imagine a dinner party where the guests devour everything in sight and then some.

8

THE AVERAGE WOLF'S FOOT SIZE IS COMPARABLE TO AN ADULT HUMAN HAND, AT 4 INCHES WIDE BY 5 INCHES LONG.

Just imagine Little Red Riding Hood's famous line, "Oh, grandmother, what big hands you have!"—but this time, it's true!

A WOLF'S HEARING IS AT LEAST 16 TIMES SHARPER THAN A HUMAN'S.

They can hear a sound as far as six miles away in the forest and ten miles away in open country. Their keen senses make them the ultimate night watchers.

 BEWARE THE BITE OF THE NIGHT!

With a jaw-crushing power of nearly 1,500 pounds per square inch, twice that of a German Shepherd, wolves are equipped with the ultimate tool for bringing down their prey.

 WOLVES CAN SWIM UP TO 8 MILES, EFFORTLESSLY GLIDING THROUGH THE WATER LIKE DARK, SLEEK SHADOWS.

 WOLVES USE FACIAL EXPRESSIONS TO DISPLAY AGGRESSION, FEAR, DOMINANCE, AND SUBMISSION.

Their expressive faces tell stories of the wild, where every glance can mean life or death.

 WOLF PUPS ARE BORN WITH BLUE EYES, WHICH CHANGE TO YELLOW-GOLD BY THE TIME THEY ARE 8-16 WEEKS OLD.

OCEAN GHOULS

1 **THE VAMPIRE SQUID GETS ITS NAME FROM ITS DARK COLOR AND RED EYES. BUT DON'T LET THE NAME FOOL YOU—IT'S NOT A SQUID AT ALL!**

Living in the deep ocean at depths of 2,000 to 3,000 feet, where sunlight never reaches, the darkness resembles a haunted abyss. This eerie creature can turn itself inside out, pulling its webbed arms over its body to hide, resembling a floating cloak of shadows.

2 **THE LAMPREY IS A PREHISTORIC, PARASITIC FISH THAT COULD STAR IN A HORROR FILM.**

It detects vibrations in the water, then latches onto its prey, feeding on flesh or sucking blood. Its round, toothed mouth is like a real-life underwater vampire.

3 **WITH ITS BRIGHT RED 'FANGS,' THE RED-TOOTHED TRIGGERFISH LOOKS READY FOR A HALLOWEEN PARTY.**

Don't worry, though. It's all gun and no bullet, making it a harmless yet spookily dressed sea dweller.

4 **IMAGINE A WORM THAT WAITS IN THE SAND WITH ONLY A FEW INCHES EXPOSED. BUT ONCE YOU PULL IT OUT, YOU REALIZE IT'S A 10-FOOT-LONG MONSTER!**

Meet the bobbit worm, a creature straight out of a nightmare.

5 **THE *TURRITOPSIS DOHRNII* JELLYFISH IS OFFICIALLY KNOWN AS THE ONLY IMMORTAL CREATURE IN THE WORLD.**

It lives forever, regenerating itself in a cycle that defies death.

6 **THE *CYMOTHOA EXIGUA*, OR "TONGUE-EATING LOUSE," ENTERS A FISH'S GILLS AND ATTACHES TO ITS TONGUE, DIVERTING BLOOD UNTIL THE TONGUE DIES.**

It then latches onto the stump, drinking blood and mucus. The worst part? The fish doesn't die and must live with its parasitic new tongue.

7 **HAGFISH ARE NOTORIOUSLY DISGUSTING, PRODUCING COPIOUS AMOUNTS OF MILKY, FIBROUS MUCUS TO EVADE OR SUFFOCATE PREDATORS.**

They can fill a five-gallon bucket with slime in minutes. To avoid suffocating in their own goo, they "sneeze" to clear their nostrils and tie themselves into knots to keep slime off their heads.

8 **GOBLIN SHARKS ARE REAL AND OFTEN REFERRED TO AS "LIVING FOSSILS."**

They are an ancient species with unique protruding jaws and fang-like teeth, giving them a truly nightmarish appearance.

9 **THE OCEAN ITSELF IS A MONSTER.**

Its depths can crush and melt humans, making it a truly terrifying force of nature.

10 **THE GIANT SQUID CAN GROW UP TO 43 FEET LONG, WITH HUGE EYES AND LONG TENTACLES LINED WITH SUCKERS.**

This colossal creature is the stuff of legends and deep-sea horror stories.

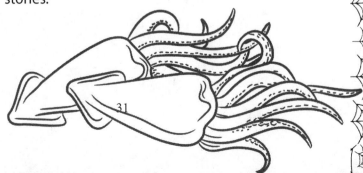

11 **THE BARRELEYE FISH HAS A TRANSPARENT HEAD AND TUBULAR EYES THAT CAN ROTATE, MAKING IT LOOK LIKE A CREATURE FROM ANOTHER WORLD.**

This fish was first identified in 1939 at depths of 2,000 to 2,600 feet and continues to fascinate and terrify.

12 **THE BLACK SWALLOWER *(CHIASMODON NIGER)* IS CAPABLE OF SWALLOWING PREY LARGER THAN ITSELF, THANKS TO ITS LARGE, DISTENSIBLE STOMACH.**

Living at depths of up to 10,000 feet, this fish is a real-life monster capable of feats that defy the imagination.

13 **ANGLERFISH LIVE IN THE DEEP OCEAN, WHERE IT'S SO DARK THAT THEIR BIOLUMINESCENT LURES ARE CRUCIAL FOR ATTRACTING PREY.**

But here's the spooky twist: some anglerfish can swallow prey twice their own size, thanks to their flexible stomachs and jaws.

SPOOKY CRITTERS

1 **A COCKROACH CAN LIVE FOR OVER A WEEK WITHOUT ITS HEAD UNTIL IT DIES OF THIRST.**

2 **THE ASIAN VAMPIRE MOTH SOMETIMES DRINKS THE BLOOD OF ANIMALS.**

These moths are real-life vampires in the insect world!

3 **CHICKENS CAN SPONTANEOUSLY CHANGE SEX FROM FEMALE TO MALE.**

Talk about some spooky farmyard magic!

4 **BEES CAN GET HOOKED ON ADDICTIVE SUBSTANCES LIKE CAFFEINE AND NICOTINE. BUZZED BEES, INDEED!**

5 **THE STING OF THE JAPANESE GIANT HORNET IS SO PAINFUL THAT IT'S NICKNAMED "MURDER HORNET."**

One sting can even cause kidney failure.

6 **BRAIN-EATING AMOEBAS EXIST AND LIVE IN WARM FRESHWATER.**

Just when you thought it was safe to go swimming.

7 **HORNED LIZARDS CAN SHOOT BLOOD FROM THEIR EYES TO SCARE OFF PREDATORS.**

Now, that's a gory defense mechanism!

FRESHWATER SNAILS KILL UP TO 20,000 PEOPLE A YEAR WITH THEIR PARASITIC INFECTIONS.

 A SLOTH'S LONG NAILS AREN'T ACTUALLY NAILS.
They're bones that protrude from the skin and are wrapped in a keratin layer. Creepy, right?

 CROWS ARE SO INTELLIGENT THEY CAN RECOGNIZE HUMAN FACES.

 LADYBUGS ARE KNOWN TO EAT THEIR OWN LARVAE TO ENSURE THE SURVIVAL OF OTHERS.
Now, that's what we call selfless, or is it?

 SOME ANTS TURN INTO ZOMBIES VIA PARASITIC FUNGUS THAT MANIPULATES THEIR BRAINS.
Zombie ants, anyone?

CHAPTER 2

HAUNTING WHISPERS

AND

CHILLING TALES

What do a creaky old house and a dusty, forgotten mirror have in common? They both might be hiding a ghost or two!

In this chapter, we'll explore haunted locations that echo with eerie whispers, cursed objects that seem to have a life of their own, and spooky stories that straddle the line between chilling and chuckling.

Ready to uncover the secrets that lie just beneath the surface? Just remember—if something goes bump in the night, it's probably just the wind... or is it?

SPINE-CHILLING SPOTS

1 **THE TOWER OF LONDON, LOCATED IN LONDON, ENGLAND, HAS A RICH HISTORY AS A ROYAL PALACE, PRISON, AND EXECUTION SITE.**

It is believed to be haunted by Anne Boleyn, who was beheaded in 1536. Her ghost is said to roam the grounds carrying her head.

2 **THE WINCHESTER MYSTERY HOUSE IN SAN JOSE, CALIFORNIA, WAS BUILT BY SARAH WINCHESTER.**

It features staircases to nowhere and doors opening into walls, believed to be designed to confuse spirits.

3 **THE AMITYVILLE HOUSE IN AMITYVILLE, NEW YORK, IS KNOWN FOR THE 1974 FAMILY MURDERS.**

It is reputed to be haunted by mysterious voices and moving objects.

4 **THE STANLEY HOTEL, LOCATED IN ESTES PARK, COLORADO, INSPIRED STEPHEN KING'S "THE SHINING."**

Guests report seeing ghostly children and hearing piano music, which is attributed to Flora Stanley's spirit.

5 **THE MOUNDSVILLE PENITENTIARY IN WEST VIRGINIA, ONE OF AMERICA'S MOST VIOLENT PRISONS FOR OVER 100 YEARS, HOUSED NEARLY 1,000 CRIMINALS UNTIL ITS CLOSURE IN 1995.**

Today, it is said that the tortured spirits of former inmates still haunt the prison, making appearances on tours.

6 **THE MYRTLES PLANTATION IN ST. FRANCISVILLE, LOUISIANA, IS A HISTORIC ANTEBELLUM HOME.**

The plantation is rumored to be haunted by ghostly children, a haunted mirror, and apparitions of formerly enslaved people.

7 **THE QUEEN MARY, DOCKED IN LONG BEACH, CALIFORNIA, IS A RETIRED OCEAN LINER BELIEVED TO BE HAUNTED BY GHOSTLY FIGURES IN THE SHIP'S POOL AND MYSTERIOUS KNOCKING SOUNDS.**

8 **THE LIZZIE BORDEN HOUSE IN FALL RIVER, MASSACHUSETTS, IS THE SITE OF THE INFAMOUS 1892 AXE MURDERS.**

Visitors claim to see apparitions of Lizzie Borden and her murdered parents.

9 **THE VILLISCA AXE MURDER HOUSE IN VILLISCA, IOWA, IS KNOWN FOR THE UNSOLVED 1912 MASS MURDER.**

Guests report ghostly voices and unexplained movements.

10 **THE BANFF SPRINGS HOTEL IN BANFF, ALBERTA, CANADA, IS A HISTORIC LUXURY HOTEL BELIEVED TO BE HAUNTED BY A BRIDE WHO DIED ON HER WEDDING DAY AND A HELPFUL BELLMAN WHO ASSISTS GUESTS FROM BEYOND THE GRAVE.**

11 **ISLA DE LAS MUÑECAS, OR THE "ISLAND OF THE DOLLS," IS ONE OF THE MOST HAUNTED PLACES IN THE WORLD.**

Creepy dolls hang from the trees, left by a man who believed they could ward off evil spirits.

12 THE ZOROASTRIANS LEAVE THEIR DEAD IN SPECIAL TOWERS CALLED "TOWERS OF SILENCE" TO BE EATEN BY VULTURES.

This ancient practice is both eerie and eco-friendly.

13 THE "DEVIL'S BIBLE," ALSO KNOWN AS THE CODEX GIGAS, IS A GIANT MEDIEVAL MANUSCRIPT SAID TO BE A CONTRACT BETWEEN A MONK AND SATAN.

Legend says the monk made a pact to write it overnight in exchange for his soul.

14 DECORATIONS MADE FROM HUMAN BONES ADORN THE INTERIOR OF THE SEDLEC OSSUARY IN THE CZECH REPUBLIC.

Over 40,000 skeletons create eerie chandeliers, pyramids, and other macabre decorations.

15 THE MÜTTER MUSEUM IN PHILADELPHIA DISPLAYS VARIOUS MUTATIONS, TUMORS, AND ANOMALIES IN HUMAN ANATOMY.

16 THE VENT HAVEN MUSEUM HOUSES VINTAGE VENTRILOQUIST DUMMIES.

These eerie dolls stare back at you with their lifelike eyes, making it feel like they might start talking on their own.

17 MUSEO DELLE ANIME DEL PURGATORIO IN ROME DISPLAYS DOCUMENTS AND ARTIFACTS OF DECEASED PEOPLE.

HALLOWEEN TALES

1 **HALLOWEEN TRACES ITS ROOTS TO THE ANCIENT CELTIC FESTIVAL OF SAMHAIN, CELEBRATED ON OCTOBER 31.**

The Celts believed this was the night when the boundary between the living and the dead was blurred.

2 **IN THE 8TH CENTURY, POPE GREGORY III DESIGNATED NOVEMBER 1 AS ALL SAINTS' DAY, A TIME TO HONOR ALL SAINTS AND MARTYRS.**

The evening before became known as All Hallows' Eve, eventually Halloween.

3 **THE TRADITION OF CARVING PUMPKINS COMES FROM AN IRISH MYTH ABOUT STINGY JACK, WHO TRICKED THE DEVIL AND WAS DOOMED TO WANDER THE EARTH WITH A CARVED-OUT TURNIP LANTERN.**

When Irish immigrants came to America, they found pumpkins more plentiful.

4 **IN MEDIEVAL EUROPE, PEOPLE DRESSED UP IN COSTUMES AND WENT DOOR-TO-DOOR, ASKING FOR FOOD IN EXCHANGE FOR PRAYERS FOR THE DEAD.**

This practice evolved into modern trick-or-treating.

5 **THE NEW YORK VILLAGE HALLOWEEN PARADE IN GREENWICH VILLAGE IS THE LARGEST IN THE WORLD, WITH 50,000 COSTUMED PARTICIPANTS AND 2 MILLION SPECTATORS.**

6 **WHILE BONFIRES ARE LINKED TO BONFIRE NIGHT TRADITIONALLY, THEY'RE ALSO COMMON AT HALLOWEEN.**

Original Celtic bonfires were called 'bone fires' because the Celts threw animal bones into the flames to ward off evil spirits.

7 **MOST LIT JACK O'LANTERNS RECORD**

The city of Keene in New Hampshire holds the Guinness World Record for the most lit Jack O'Lanterns on display, with a record of 30,581.

8 **THE LOUDEST SCREAM**

Classroom assistant Jill Drake (UK) had a scream that reached 129 dBA at the Halloween festivities held in the Millennium Dome, London, in October 2000.

9 **THE LARGEST PUMPKIN SCULPTURE**

The largest pumpkin sculpture, depicting a zombie apocalypse, used two pumpkins weighing 1,818 lb and 1,693 lb and took two days to complete.

10 **A TRADITION IN GERMANY IS TO HIDE ALL YOUR KNIVES ON HALLOWEEN.**

11 **IT IS ILLEGAL TO DRESS AS A NUN OR PRIEST IN ALABAMA.**

If caught, you could face a fine or even be arrested.

12 **THE HIGHEST NUMBER OF PEOPLE DRESSED AS GHOSTS IN ONE LOCATION WAS 560 ON MARCH 24, 2017.**

13 THE LARGEST HAUNTED HOUSE

In 2015, Guinness World Records named Cutting Edge Haunted House in Fort Worth, Texas, the "World's Largest Walkthrough Haunted House." It is built inside an abandoned meat packing factory.

14 THE LARGEST CORN MAZE

The world's largest temporary corn maze covered 60 acres and was made in Dixon, California, in 2014.

15 THE AVERAGE AMERICAN WILL EAT AROUND 3.4 LB OF CANDY ON HALLOWEEN.

16 IN 2014, THERE WERE 15,458 PEOPLE DRESSED UP AS ZOMBIES IN MINNEAPOLIS, MINNESOTA, USA.

17 IN ANCIENT ENGLAND, PEOPLE USED HOLLOWED HUMAN SKULLS AS BOWLS AND CUPS.

Drinking from a skull was believed to bring the drinker the power and wisdom of the deceased.

18 ROMAN EMPEROR NERO PROFITED OFF OF HUMAN URINE BY TAXING PUBLIC URINALS.

The urine was used in various ancient Roman industries, including laundry and tanning.

19 DURING MUMMIFICATION, ANCIENT EGYPTIANS REMOVED THE BRAIN THROUGH ONE OF THE NOSTRILS.

CURSED COLLECTIBLES

1

THE HOPE DIAMOND
This 45.52-carat blue diamond is believed to carry a curse, bringing misfortune and tragedy to its owners. It is now displayed in the Smithsonian Institution.

2

ANNABELLE DOLL
This Raggedy Ann doll is said to be possessed by an evil spirit and is kept in a glass case at the Warren's Occult Museum in Connecticut.

3

ROBERT THE DOLL
Believed to be cursed, Robert the Doll is housed at the Fort East Martello Museum in Florida. Visitors claim to experience misfortune after photographing it without permission.

4

THE DYBBUK BOX
A wine cabinet said to be haunted by a malicious spirit from Jewish folklore. Its owners have reported strange occurrences and bad luck.

5

BUSBY'S STOOP CHAIR
This wooden chair, owned by convicted murderer Thomas Busby, is believed to bring death to anyone who sits in it. It is now displayed in the Thirsk Museum in England, hung high on a wall to prevent use.

6 THE MYRTLES PLANTATION MIRROR

Located in Louisiana, this mirror is believed to hold the spirits of Sara Woodruff and her children, who were poisoned on the plantation.

7 JAMES DEAN'S CURSED CAR

The actor's Porsche 550 Spyder, nicknamed "Little Bastard," is believed to be cursed after causing his fatal accident and subsequent mishaps for others.

8 THE BASANO VASE

An Italian silver vase from the 15th century, believed to be cursed after causing the deaths of several owners. It was reportedly buried to stop the curse.

9 THE CRYING BOY PAINTING

A mass-produced print of a crying boy, said to bring house fires to its owners. Despite many incidents, the paintings often survive the fires unscathed.

10 THE CONJURE CHEST

A wooden chest from the 19th century, believed to be cursed by an enslaved woman. Many of its owners reportedly experienced tragedy and death.

SPECTRAL CELEBRATIONS

1 HUNGRY GHOST FESTIVAL

Celebrated in China and East Asia during the seventh lunar month, it's believed that ghosts return to the living world. Families offer food and burn incense to appease them.

2 OBON FESTIVAL

A Japanese Buddhist tradition held in August, where lanterns are lit to guide ancestors' spirits back to their resting places.

3 PITRU PAKSHA

A Hindu festival in India, observed in September, where people offer food and prayers to their ancestors.

4 CHUSEOK

A Korean harvest festival in September, where families honor their ancestors with food offerings and rituals.

5 GAI JATRA

Celebrated in Nepal, this festival involves a procession of cows to guide the souls of the deceased to the afterlife.

6 DIA DE LOS MUERTOS

In Mexico, celebrated on November 1st and 2nd, families create ofrendas (altars) with food, flowers, and photos to honor deceased loved ones.

7 TẾT TRUNG NGUYÊN

In Vietnam, the Ghost Festival is held on the 15th day of the seventh lunar month, with food offerings and burning paper money for wandering spirits.

8 ALL SAINTS' DAY AND ALL SOULS' DAY

Observed in many Christian countries on November 1st and 2nd, these days honor all saints and the souls of the faithful departed.

9 PCHUM BEN

A Cambodian festival held in September or October, where people pay respects to their ancestors through food offerings at temples.

10 JINGZHE (AWAKENING OF INSECTS)

In China, this festival marks the beginning of spring in March. People believe this is the time of the year when spirits and insects awaken from their winter slumber.

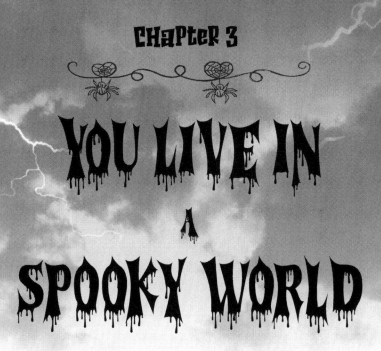

CHAPTER 3

YOU LIVE IN A SPOOKY WORLD

The world is full of surprises—some that leave us in awe, and others that send shivers down our spines. Imagine living in a world where supervolcanoes could erupt without warning, blanketing the sky in ash, or where a massive tsunami could wipe out entire coastlines in a single sweep.

In this chapter, we'll explore just how lucky we are to be here, navigating a planet filled with hidden dangers. Every day, we're dancing on the edge, balancing between the wonders of nature and its terrifying potential.

So, let's dive into the forces that shape our world—and the lurking threats that keep us on our toes.

SURVIVING AGAINST ALL ODDS

1 **THERE ARE ABOUT 40 SUPERVOLCANOES WORLDWIDE CAPABLE OF CAUSING CATASTROPHIC DAMAGE, POTENTIALLY AFFECTING UP TO A BILLION LIVES.**

To make it worse, we are approximately 24,000 years overdue for an eruption.

2 **YOU CAN LITERALLY THINK YOURSELF TO DEATH.**

If you believe strongly enough that you have been cursed, your brain can shut itself off entirely in severe cases. The psychological term for it is "Voodoo Death Syndrome."

3 THE EARTH CAN BE HIT WITH A GAMMA-RAY BURST AT ANY GIVEN TIME.

It is so powerful that it could sterilize all life on Earth — or even vaporize the planet. Luckily, the chances of one happening in our solar system are slim.

4 THE DEADLIEST TORNADO

The deadliest tornado in U.S. history, the Tri-State Tornado of 1925, traveled 219 miles across Missouri, Illinois, and Indiana, killing 695 people.

5 THE BLISSFUL EIGHT

If the sun exploded right now, you would be blissfully unaware of it for just over eight minutes while the energy travels at the speed of light to get to you.

6 IN 1952, LONDON WAS SHROUDED IN A "GREAT KILLER FOG" THAT LASTED FIVE DAYS AND RESULTED IN THE DEATHS OF AN ESTIMATED 4,000 PEOPLE.

The deadly smog was caused by severe air pollution, primarily from coal burning.

7 A MEGA-TSUNAMI COULD BRING ABOUT THE END OF THE WORLD.

It has happened before, causing massive destruction and possibly contributing to the dinosaurs' extinction. It could happen again, and there's nothing we can do to stop it.

8 RIP CURRENTS CAN DRAG YOU OUT TO SEA.

To make matters worse, we humans are biologically attracted to its shiny depths.

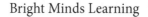

THE CARRINGTON EVENT WAS A LARGE SOLAR STORM THAT TOOK PLACE AT THE BEGINNING OF SEPTEMBER 1859.

It was so powerful that telegraph operators reported sparks flying from their equipment, and some telegraph paper caught fire. Imagine communication lines seemingly possessed by ghostly forces!

SPACE WEATHER CAN SOMETIMES CAUSE UNEXPLAINED ATMOSPHERIC NOISES, KNOWN AS "SKYQUAKES" OR "MYSTERY BOOMS."

These loud sounds add an eerie element to geomagnetic storms, though their exact causes remain unclear.

ONE ROCK HURTLING THROUGH SPACE CAN DESTROY HUMANITY.

Debris is common in space. While most are innocuous to individuals on Earth, it only takes a 0.6-mile-wide boulder to endanger the survival of our entire race. Even smaller rocks, measuring about 130 feet across, can cause catastrophic damage to the planet.

DID YOU KNOW A SUNBURN IS ACTUALLY A RADIATION BURN?

UV rays from the sun damage your skin's proteins, membranes, and DNA. This stops accurate DNA replication, so cells start repairing to fix the mistakes. Too many DNA errors overwhelm the cell and cause it to self-destruct, removing cells that can't be safely replicated.

DANCING WITH DANGER

1 **ANCIENT VIRUSES**

Ancient viruses frozen in the Arctic permafrost could one day be released by Earth's warming climate and unleash a major disease outbreak.

2 **IF YOU'RE EXPOSED TO RABIES AND START TO SHOW SYMPTOMS, YOUR CHANCE OF SURVIVAL IS VIRTUALLY ZERO PERCENT.**

This terrifying virus can turn the simplest animal bite into a death sentence.

3 **HEART MUSCLE CELLS REPRODUCE LESS THAN 1% PER YEAR.**

So, if you damage your heart, those cells won't be replaced. It's like having a fragile, ticking time bomb inside your chest.

4 **ACCORDING TO THE WORLD HEALTH ORGANIZATION (WHO), APPROXIMATELY 25% OF THE WORLD'S POPULATION HAS AN INFECTION RELATED TO AN INTESTINAL PARASITE.**

In tropical and subtropical areas with limited access to clean water and sanitation, that number is as high as 50%.

5 **SEA WATER LEVELS ARE RISING AT AN ALARMING RATE, MAINLY CAUSED BY THE MELTING OF ARCTIC SEA ICE.**

YOUR EYES HAVE THEIR OWN IMMUNE SYSTEM THAT WORKS SEPARATELY FROM YOUR BODY'S IMMUNE SYSTEM.

If your body's immune system finds out, it will attack your eyes.

 YOUR BRAIN IS EATING ITSELF ALL THE TIME!

 A BRAIN TRICK

When you look at a clock and the second hand seems to freeze for a moment, your brain generates a false memory – and your perception of time stretches slightly backward.

 PIGS CAN EAT AN ENTIRE HUMAN BODY, MOSTLY BECAUSE THEY'LL JUST EAT ANYTHING.

 A CELL PHONE IS MORE DISGUSTING THAN A PUBLIC TOILET.

A regular cell phone has 10 times more bacteria than the average public restroom. More books, people?

 IN 2017, A 75-YEAR-OLD WOMAN SURVIVED A TORNADO BY TAKING SHELTER IN HER BATHTUB.

The tornado ripped off her house's roof, lifted the tub with her in it, and deposited it in the woods, leaving her uninjured.

12 THE BACTERIA ON YOUR SKIN DEGRADE THE PROTEINS IN YOUR SWEAT, RESULTING IN A FOUL-SMELLING WASTE.

13 SPOOKY MEDICINE

Until the 20th century, human remains were used to make medicine.

14 CHAINSAWS WERE ORIGINALLY CREATED FOR CHILDBIRTH.

If babies were too big to pass through the birth canal, a chainsaw was used to remove parts of the pelvis quickly.

15 IN THE 1800S, DENTURES WERE MADE OUT OF THE REAL TEETH OF DECEASED PEOPLE.

16 DISNEYLAND'S RIDE ORIGINALLY USED REAL SKELETONS FROM UCLA'S ANATOMY DEPARTMENT.

As technology improved and fake skeletons began to look more authentic, the real skeletons were reportedly given a proper burial.

LIVING WITH THE PARANORMAL

1 **THE SMELL OF A FRESHLY CUT LAWN IS A CHEMICAL DISTRESS SIGNAL RELEASED FROM THE GRASS AS IT'S CUT.**

2 **THE BOTTOM OF LAKE SUPERIOR IS SO COLD THAT THE BODIES OF DEAD PEOPLE REMAIN PRESERVED.**
It's a watery graveyard where time stands still.

3 **A CHICKEN CALLED MIKE THE HEADLESS CHICKEN LIVED FOR 18 MONTHS AFTER ITS HEAD WAS CUT OFF.**

4 **THE BLOOP**
There is a mystery sound known as "The Bloop," emerging from the deepest part of the ocean. Until now, the exact cause of the sound remains unknown.

5 **TITANIC PREDICTION**
A book written 14 years before the 1912 sinking of the Titanic may have predicted the ship's tragic demise. Coincidence?

6 **IN 1915, 30-YEAR-OLD ESSIE DUNBAR WAS DECLARED DEAD AFTER AN EPILEPSY ATTACK.**
She was buried the following morning, but her sister asked to dig up the coffin so she could see her sister one last time. When the coffin opened, Essie sat up and smiled. She went on to live another 47 years, although many people believed her to be a zombie.

? THE WALLS OF BONES

The Catacombs of Paris hold the remains of more than six million people. Its walls are also made of bones.

8 REAL-LIFE VAMPIRES?

In ancient Rome, people used to believe that drinking the blood of dead gladiators would give them strength. The ancient Romans also thought drinking blood would cure epilepsy.

9 THE SILENT SCREAM

Some plants make ultrasonic sounds when stressed, especially when they are dehydrated or have their leaves chopped. These noises are too powerful for humans to perceive but may be detected using specialized technology.

10 THE DREAMY SIX

Individuals spend nearly one-third of their lives sleeping, with an average of two hours of dreaming per night. For an average person, this amounts to six years spent dreaming.

11 THE BERMUDA TRIANGLE

The Bermuda Triangle, located in the western Atlantic Ocean, has historically been linked to inexplicable disappearances of ships and planes.

A CUBIC MILE OF FOG COMPRISES AROUND 56,000 GALLONS OF WATER.

 FISH RAIN

Tornadoes and waterspouts have been known to pick up fish from bodies of water and drop them miles away, causing "fish rain." In 2010, residents of the small town of Lajamanu in Australia's Northern Territory experienced a bizarre weather event where fish rained from the sky.

 AN UNSOLVED MYSTERY: THE HUM

The Hum is a persistent, low-frequency noise heard by approximately 2-4% of the global population. Sufferers report health issues such as headaches, nausea, and insomnia, but the exact cause remains unknown.

 SQUEAKY BEACH

On the Squeaky Beach in Victoria, Australia, the quartz sand grains produce a distinctive whistling sound when walked on.

CHAPTER 4

BOO-TIFUL FRIGHTS

AND

FUN DELIGHTS

Who says fear can't be fun? Whether it's jumping out of your skin at a haunted house or laughing at the creepy crawlies that make your hair stand on end, there's a thrill in the chill!

In this chapter, we'll explore the funny side of fear, where goosebumps meet giggles. From flowers that look more like monsters to the quirky ways we've turned terror into tradition, get ready to embrace the spooky and the spectacular with a smile on your face.

THE THRILL OF THE CHILL

1 ### THE ADRENALINE RUSH

When we experience fear, our body releases adrenaline, heightening our senses and providing a thrilling rush similar to the excitement of extreme sports or a roller coaster ride. This adrenaline release can sometimes even enable superhuman feats, like lifting cars or escaping dangerous situations.

2 ### RUNNER'S HIGH

Fear triggers the release of endorphins and dopamine, our body's natural feel-good chemicals, making us feel like we've just run a marathon or eaten a giant chocolate bar. It's a bit like the "runner's high," but without the sweaty sneakers!

3 ### THE THRILL OF DANGER

People enjoy being scared in controlled environments like haunted houses or horror movies, where they know they are safe from actual harm. It's the thrill of danger. Haunted attractions in the U.S. alone generate over $300 million in revenue per year.

4 **OUR BRAINS LOVE NEW EXPERIENCES, AND SPOOKY ACTIVITIES PROVIDE JUST THAT.**

It's like opening a mystery box, except the surprise inside might make you scream (in a fun way).

5 **WE NEEDED FEAR TO SURVIVE.**

Our ancestors needed fear to survive, like running away from saber-toothed tigers. Now, we get the same thrill from spooky stories, which are much safer and involve fewer sharp teeth.

6 **FACING SOMETHING SCARY AND COMING OUT UNSCATHED CAN BE INCREDIBLY SATISFYING.**

Fear increases heart rate and alertness, making us feel alive and energized. It's like drinking a supercharged energy drink but with a side of spookiness.

? **EXPERIENCING FEAR CAN HELP RELEASE PENT-UP EMOTIONS, HELPING PEOPLE PURGE NEGATIVE FEELINGS IN A SAFE AND CONTROLLED WAY.**

8 THE SAME PART OF THE BRAIN THAT REACTS TO FEAR, THE AMYGDALA, ALSO RESPONDS TO HAPPINESS.

Interestingly, this dual role means that the amygdala can amplify a roller coaster's thrill and the joy of a surprise party.

9 THE FIGHT-OR-FLIGHT RESPONSE CAN PUT YOU ON HIGH ALERT.

You might jump if you catch your reflection out of the corner of your eye in a dark hallway — your brain detects a potential threat. It reacts within milliseconds, even before you consciously realize there's no danger.

10 SOME PEOPLE FREEZE IN FEAR, LIKE WHEN SEEING A BEAR, INSTEAD OF RUNNING AWAY.

Getting used to controlled scares, such as Halloween haunted houses, can help you adapt and become more resilient. Plus, it might save you from being a bear's snack!

WHEN FEAR TAKES OVER

1 **FEAR CAUSES OUR HEART RATE TO SPIKE, PUMPING MORE BLOOD TO MUSCLES AND VITAL ORGANS AND PREPARING OUR BODY FOR RAPID ACTIONS.**

This heightened alertness is crucial for survival, enabling quick reactions and increased strength. For example, the sudden boost in blood flow can help us sprint away from danger or confront a threat head-on with greater force.

2 **WHEN WE ARE SCARED, OUR PUPILS DILATE TO ALLOW MORE LIGHT INTO THE EYES, IMPROVING VISION AND MAKING US MORE AWARE OF OUR SURROUNDINGS.**

In low-light conditions, dilated pupils can significantly enhance our night vision, which is essential for detecting dark threats.

3 **FEAR TRIGGERS SWEATING TO COOL THE BODY DOWN AND PREVENT OVERHEATING DURING INTENSE PHYSICAL ACTIVITY.**

This is why we often feel clammy when scared.

4 **OUR SENSES BECOME SHARPER, AND THE BRAIN BECOMES MORE ALERT WHEN WE ARE SCARED.**

This hyper-awareness helps us detect and respond to threats more effectively.

5 **BUTTERFLIES IN THE STOMACH**

Digestive processes slow down or halt as the body prioritizes energy for immediate survival rather than digestion. This can lead to the sensation of "butterflies" in the stomach.

6 FEAR CAUSES OUR BREATHING RATE TO INCREASE TO SUPPLY MORE OXYGEN TO THE BODY.

This ensures that our muscles have the energy they need for quick movements.

? EXTREME HEARING

Sometimes, intense fear can cause auditory exclusion, making our hearing less sensitive to background noise. This helps us focus on the immediate threat.

8 GOOSEBUMPS

Fear can cause the tiny muscles at the base of hair follicles to contract, creating goosebumps. This reaction is a remnant of our ancestors' need to appear larger to predators.

9 SALIVA PRODUCTION DECREASES DURING A FEAR RESPONSE, LEADING TO A DRY MOUTH.

This happens because the body diverts fluids to other areas needed for survival.

10 IN EXTREME CASES, FEAR CAN CAUSE A LOSS OF BLADDER OR BOWEL CONTROL.

This is due to the body's intense focus on immediate survival, sometimes at the expense of other functions.

THRIVING THROUGH TERROR

1 **SOME ANIMALS, LIKE DEER AND RABBITS, FREEZE WHEN THEY SENSE DANGER.**

This reaction makes them less noticeable to predators, like turning into a furry statue in the middle of a spooky forest.

2 **CERTAIN ANIMALS USE CAMOUFLAGE TO BLEND INTO THEIR SURROUNDINGS WHEN THEY ARE SCARED.**

Chameleons can change color to hide from predators, making them the ultimate hide-and-seek champions.

3 **OPOSSUMS ARE FAMOUS FOR "PLAYING DEAD" WHEN THREATENED.**

This behavior, called thanatosis, can deter predators who prefer live prey, like a zombie tricking its pursuers.

4 **SKUNKS RELEASE A FOUL-SMELLING SPRAY TO WARD OFF PREDATORS WHEN THEY FEEL THREATENED.**

This powerful defense mechanism can deter even the most persistent attackers, like a natural stink bomb.

5 **THE KING SNAKE IS NON-VENOMOUS BUT HAS BRIGHT RED, YELLOW, AND BLACK BANDS, MAKING IT LOOK LIKE A DANGEROUS CORAL SNAKE.**

This helps it avoid predators. When it feels scared, the king snake will coil up, hiss, and shake its tail to act like a rattlesnake, scaring away any threats.

6 **ANIMALS LIKE COBRAS AND FRILLED LIZARDS USE INTIMIDATION DISPLAYS TO SCARE OFF PREDATORS.**

Cobras spread their hoods, while frilled lizards display their neck frills and hiss like monsters puffing up to look scarier.

7 **SOME AMPHIBIANS, LIKE POISON DART FROGS, SECRETE TOXINS THROUGH THEIR SKIN TO DETER PREDATORS.**

These chemicals can be deadly if ingested, making them the venomous villains of the forest.

8 **BIRDS LIKE KILLDEER FEIGN INJURY TO LURE PREDATORS AWAY FROM THEIR NESTS.**

They pretend to have a broken wing, leading the predator away from their chicks, like a dramatic performance in a spooky play.

9 **OCTOPUSES USE INK CLOUDS TO OBSCURE THEIR ESCAPE WHEN THREATENED.**

This tactic confuses predators, allowing the octopus to flee like a ninja disappearing in a puff of smoke.

10 **ELEPHANTS USE VOCALIZATIONS LIKE TRUMPETING TO WARN THE HERD OF DANGER, PRODUCING SOUNDS THAT CAN BE INCREDIBLY LOUD.**

These trumpeting calls can reach up to 112 decibels, about as loud as a rock concert. Elephants' calls can be heard over several miles, alerting other elephants to the threat.

FLOWERS WITH A DARK SIDE

1 THE VENUS FLYTRAP IS A CARNIVOROUS PLANT THAT SNAPS SHUT ON ITS PREY, SUCH AS INSECTS, WITH LIGHTNING-FAST SPEED.

Its trap can close in less than a second, and the plant then secretes digestive enzymes to consume its meal.

2 ALSO KNOWN AS MONKSHOOD OR WOLF'S BANE, ACONITE IS A HIGHLY TOXIC PLANT.

Historically, it was used to poison arrows and was believed to repel werewolves and witches. Even small amounts can cause serious health issues if ingested.

3 PITCHER PLANTS HAVE DEEP, PITCHER-SHAPED LEAVES FILLED WITH DIGESTIVE LIQUID.

Unsuspecting insects and even small animals like frogs can fall into these traps, where they are digested by the plant. Some species have pitchers that can hold over two liters of fluid.

 4 THE GHOST ORCHID IS NAMED FOR ITS GHOSTLY APPEARANCE, WITH PALE WHITE FLOWERS THAT SEEM TO FLOAT IN THE AIR.

It has no leaves and relies on photosynthesis through its roots. It is extremely rare and can only be found in specific swampy areas in Florida and Cuba.

 5 THE SEED PODS OF DEVIL'S CLAW HAVE LONG, CURVED HOOKS THAT LATCH ONTO ANIMALS' FUR OR HUMANS' CLOTHING.

This plant was used by Native Americans for its medicinal properties, and its hooks look like spooky claws.

 6 THE CORPSE FLOWER IS FAMOUS FOR ITS PUTRID SMELL, RESEMBLING THAT OF ROTTING FLESH.

This odor attracts pollinators like carrion beetles and flies. It is one of the largest flowers in the world and can reach up to 10 feet tall.

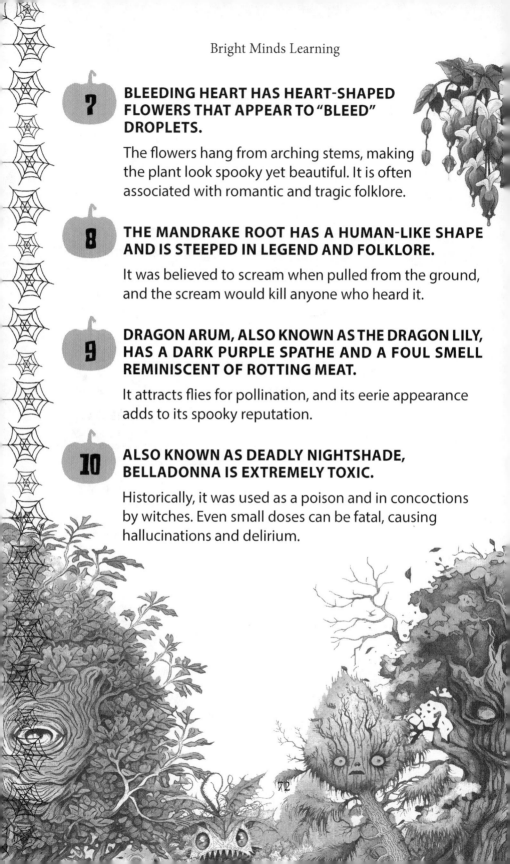

7 **BLEEDING HEART HAS HEART-SHAPED FLOWERS THAT APPEAR TO "BLEED" DROPLETS.**

The flowers hang from arching stems, making the plant look spooky yet beautiful. It is often associated with romantic and tragic folklore.

8 **THE MANDRAKE ROOT HAS A HUMAN-LIKE SHAPE AND IS STEEPED IN LEGEND AND FOLKLORE.**

It was believed to scream when pulled from the ground, and the scream would kill anyone who heard it.

9 **DRAGON ARUM, ALSO KNOWN AS THE DRAGON LILY, HAS A DARK PURPLE SPATHE AND A FOUL SMELL REMINISCENT OF ROTTING MEAT.**

It attracts flies for pollination, and its eerie appearance adds to its spooky reputation.

10 **ALSO KNOWN AS DEADLY NIGHTSHADE, BELLADONNA IS EXTREMELY TOXIC.**

Historically, it was used as a poison and in concoctions by witches. Even small doses can be fatal, causing hallucinations and delirium.

EVEN HUMANS CAN BE CREEPY

1 **YOUR EYES ARE AN EXPOSED EXTENSION OF YOUR BRAIN, DIRECTLY CONNECTED THROUGH THE OPTIC NERVE.**

This connection allows your brain to process the visual information your eyes capture, making them essential for seeing and interpreting the world around you.

2 **ON AVERAGE, A PERSON SWEATS AROUND ONE CUP PER DAY.**

That's like pouring out a small bottle of sweat daily, which helps cool your body and remove toxins.

3 **THE FLOATING SPECS YOU OFTEN SEE ARE LIKELY NOT DUST BUT TINY DEAD SKIN CELLS.**

These ghostly remnants drift around, constantly shed by your body as it renews its skin.

4 **WE ALL HAVE TEENY TINY MITES LIVING ON OUR EYELASHES CALLED DEMODEX.**

These invisible companions feed on oils and dead skin cells, living their entire lives unnoticed on your face.

5 **AFTER ALBERT EINSTEIN'S DEATH, SCIENTISTS PRESERVED HIS BRAIN TO STUDY ITS UNIQUE STRUCTURE.**

6 IN THE 18TH CENTURY, DOCTORS PRACTICED BLOODLETTING, BELIEVING IT WOULD BALANCE ONE'S HEALTH.

 7 DEAD BODIES CAN STILL GET GOOSEBUMPS BECAUSE OF POSTMORTEM MUSCLE CONTRACTIONS.

Even in death, the chills can get you!

 8 HUMANS SHED SKIN CONSTANTLY, AMOUNTING TO ROUGHLY 112 POUNDS OVER A LIFETIME.

This means you shed almost an entire person's worth of skin throughout your life.

 9 IN 2009, A RUSSIAN MAN HAD A FIR TREE GROWING INSIDE HIS LUNG.

The tree was about 2 centimeters tall and had green needles.

 10 YOUR BED CAN HAVE UP TO 10 MILLION DUST MITES.

They eat your dead skin cells. Now, it's easier to change your bed sheets more often, right?

11. YOUR EARS NEVER STOP GROWING!

This happens because of gravity and the natural breakdown of collagen and elastin in the cartilage, causing them to elongate and sag as you age.

12. THE TONGUE IS COVERED IN 2,000 TO 8,000 TASTE BUDS, EACH CONTAINING UP TO 100 CELLS THAT HELP YOU TASTE YOUR FOOD.

These taste buds regenerate every one to two weeks, keeping your sense of taste sharp.

13. YOU ARE SLIGHTLY TALLER IN THE MORNING THAN AT NIGHT BECAUSE YOUR SPINE DECOMPRESSES WHILE YOU SLEEP.

As the day progresses, gravity compresses your spine, making you a bit shorter by bedtime.

14. SPOOKY PEANUT BUTTER

Arachibutyrophobia is the fear of peanut butter actually getting stuck on the roof of your mouth, which can give some people the feeling of "choking."

CHAPTER 5

ARE YOU GONNA EAT THAT?

Ready to sink your teeth into something spooky? In this chapter, we're diving into the world of foods that are as frightening as they are fascinating.

From desserts that might bite back to snacks that send shivers down your spine, we'll explore the eerie edibles that make your taste buds tingle and your hair stand on end.

So grab a fork (or maybe some garlic) and get ready to feast on the weird, wild, and wonderfully creepy side of food!

AGED AND AWFUL

1

IMAGINE A HALLOWEEN SNACK THAT SMELLS LIKE IT'S BEEN LEFT OUT SINCE LAST YEAR'S PARTY!

Stinky tofu is a popular treat in China and Taiwan, and it is known for its super strong smell, like rotten garbage. The tofu is soaked in a special spooky brine made from fermented milk, vegetables, and meat, making it a frightfully tasty snack.

2

THIS SWEDISH DELICACY SMELLS SO BAD IT COULD SCARE A VAMPIRE AWAY!

Known as one of the world's stinkiest foods, Surströmming is a fermented herring that's traditionally eaten outdoors. The cans can even look like they're haunted, bulging due to the ongoing fermentation process inside.

3

STICKY LIKE A SPIDER'S WEB AND SMELLING LIKE A ZOMBIE'S BREATH, NATTO IS A JAPANESE FAVORITE MADE FROM FERMENTED SOYBEANS.

It's packed with protein and probiotics, making it a super healthy treat for those brave enough to try it.

4

CALLED THE "KING OF FRUITS" BUT SMELLING LIKE THE "KING OF THE CRYPT," DURIAN HAS A STENCH COMPARED TO RAW SEWAGE AND ROTTEN ONIONS.

Despite the spooky smell, it's beloved in Southeast Asia for its creamy texture and sweet taste.

78

5 KIMCHI

This fiery Korean classic is a mix of fermented vegetables, usually cabbage and radishes, seasoned with chili pepper, garlic, and ginger.

6 WITH BLUE AND GREEN VEINS THAT LOOK LIKE THEY BELONG ON A GHOST, BLUE CHEESE IS AGED WITH A SPECIAL MOLD THAT GIVES IT A STRONG, SPOOKY FLAVOR.

Varieties like Roquefort and Stilton are loved around the world, even if they look a bit haunted.

7 KNOWN AS THE "MAGGOT CHEESE," CASU MARZU IS A SARDINIAN CHEESE FILLED WITH LIVE INSECT LARVAE.

Talking about extra protein, huh?

8 MISO IS A JAPANESE SEASONING MADE FROM FERMENTED SOYBEANS, RICE, OR BARLEY MIXED WITH A MOLD CALLED KOJI.

It's used in soups and sauces, adding a savory, umami flavor that's like a magical potion for your taste buds.

9 HÁKARL IS A FERMENTED SHARK MEAT THAT SMELLS STRONG ENOUGH TO WAKE THE DEAD!

Hákarl is buried and fermented for months before use.

10 CENTURY EGGS ARE A CHINESE DELICACY PRESERVED FOR WEEKS TO MONTHS, TRANSFORMING THEM INTO DARK, JELLY-LIKE EGGS WITH A STRONG FLAVOR.

They might look like they've been dug up from an ancient tomb, but they're a cherished treat for adventurous eaters.

RISKY SWEETS

1 KNOWN AS THE "CHOCOLATE PUDDING FRUIT," BLACK SAPOTE TASTES LIKE A DELIGHTFUL MIX OF CHOCOLATE PUDDING AND FRUIT.

It's a surprisingly sweet treat that sounds like it belongs in a candy store!

2 BELIEVE IT OR NOT, A DENTIST NAMED WILLIAM MORRISON CO-INVENTED COTTON CANDY IN 1897.

He called it "Fairy Floss," a spooky name for a treat spun from sugar that melts in your mouth like magic.

3 DESPITE ITS NAME, WHITE CHOCOLATE ISN'T REALLY CHOCOLATE BECAUSE IT DOESN'T CONTAIN COCOA SOLIDS.

It's made from cocoa butter, sugar, and milk solids, making it a sweet treat that's a bit of an impostor!

4 IT TAKES LICKING MACHINES (YES, THEY'RE REAL) ANYWHERE FROM 364 TO 411 LICKS TO REACH THE CENTER OF A TOOTSIE POP.

That's a lot of licking for a sweet surprise!

5 INSPIRED BY THE TALE OF SNOW WHITE, POISON CANDY APPLE IS A CREEPY TWIST ON THE CLASSIC TREAT.

While they aren't poisonous, their eerie black and red colors make them look like something a wicked witch might offer.

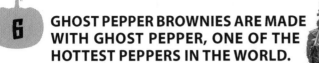

6 **GHOST PEPPER BROWNIES ARE MADE WITH GHOST PEPPER, ONE OF THE HOTTEST PEPPERS IN THE WORLD.**

Only the bravest dare to try them!

7 **DID YOU KNOW THAT CHOCOLATE-COVERED INSECTS, LIKE CRICKETS AND ANTS, ARE NOT ONLY A CRUNCHY SNACK BUT ALSO A GOOD SOURCE OF PROTEIN?**

They're enjoyed in many cultures worldwide and add a daring twist to your dessert table.

8 **BEANBOOZLED JELLY BEANS COME IN FLAVORS RANGING FROM DELICIOUS TO DISGUSTING, LIKE "STINKY SOCKS" AND "ROTTEN EGG."**

Perfect for a game where you never know if you're getting a yummy or yucky flavor.

9 **EATING 262 FUN-SIZED HALLOWEEN CANDY BARS WOULD POISON A 180-POUND PERSON.**

That's a lot of candy to turn you into a Halloween horror story!

10 **DO YOU KNOW SOME PEOPLE SAY YOUR STOMACH WILL EXPLODE IF YOU EAT POP ROCKS WITH SODA?**

The good thing is that's just a myth! But Pop Rocks is still a blast with their fizzy, popping sensation that turns your mouth into a mini fireworks show with every bite.

CREEPY CUISINE

1 **ONE FAST-FOOD HAMBURGER MAY CONTAIN MEAT FROM AS MANY AS 100 DIFFERENT COWS.**

This mixing of meat from various sources helps maintain consistent flavor and texture.

2 **RAW OYSTERS ARE STILL ALIVE WHEN YOU EAT THEM.**

Fresh and freaky!

3 **VEGAN STEAK**

Chickpeas and almonds are surprisingly high in protein, containing almost as much protein as steak.

4 **IN THE SOUTHERN UNITED STATES, ALLIGATOR MEAT IS CONSIDERED A DELICACY.**

It's often compared to chicken in flavor and texture and is typically prepared fried, grilled, or in a gumbo.

5 **IN AUSTRALIA, KANGAROO MEAT IS A POPULAR AND SUSTAINABLE OPTION.**

It's lean, high in protein, and considered more environmentally friendly than traditional livestock farming.

6 **THE HISSING CHICKEN**

Snake meat is eaten in various cultures around the world, often described as tasting like chicken.

82

7 THE BLACK LINE IN SHRIMP IS ITS INTESTINES.

8 RUN, RUN, MY LITTLE PONY!

Although controversial in some places, horse meat is considered a delicacy in countries like Japan, Italy, and France.

9 COMMONLY CONSUMED IN FRENCH CUISINE, FROG LEGS ARE SAID TO TASTE LIKE A CROSS BETWEEN CHICKEN AND FISH.

They are often sautéed, fried, or prepared in garlic butter.

10 IN CAMBODIA, PEOPLE MUNCH ON DEEP-FRIED TARANTULAS.

These eight-legged snacks are crunchy on the outside and gooey on the inside.

11 IN CANADA, SOME BRAVE SOULS ENJOY JELLIED MOOSE NOSES.

This dish is exactly what it sounds like—moose nose cooked until it turns into jelly. It's a creepy culinary adventure!

12 THE CARNIVOROUS FRUIT

Pineapples contain an enzyme called bromelain that digests protein. When you eat pineapple, this enzyme starts breaking down your mouth's proteins, so it's like it is eating you back!

PUMPKINS ARE CLASSIFIED AS A FRUIT, NOT A VEGETABLE!

 ASTRONAUT SCOTT KELLY DRANK 730 LITERS OF HIS OWN SWEAT AND URINE TO STAY HYDRATED DURING HIS YEAR IN SPACE.

It sounds gross, but it's a clever way to recycle water!

 IN THE 1800S, KETCHUP WAS SOLD AS A MEDICINE TO TREAT DIGESTIVE ISSUES.

Talk about a tasty cure!

 EVER NOTICED YOUR PEE SMELLS FUNNY AFTER EATING ASPARAGUS?

That's because asparagus contains a compound that releases a sulfurous odor when digested.

 IF CORIANDER TASTES LIKE SOAP TO YOU, BLAME YOUR GENES.

Some people have a genetic variation that makes coriander taste soapy.

 CANNED MUSHROOMS CAN LEGALLY CONTAIN A FEW MAGGOTS.

That's some unexpected extra protein!

SINISTER SNACKS

1 **DID YOU KNOW THAT GUMMY BEARS GET THEIR CHEWY TEXTURE FROM GELATIN, MADE BY BOILING PIG BONES, SKIN, AND CONNECTIVE TISSUES?**

Next time you snack on these squishy treats, remember they're a bit more "animal" than you might think.

2 **JELLY BEANS GET THEIR SHINY, HARD COATING FROM SHELLAC, A RESIN SECRETED BY THE FEMALE LAC BUG.**

That's right, your favorite colorful candy is coated in bug goop! Every year, about 15 billion jelly beans are eaten, enough to circle the Earth nearly five times if laid end to end.

3 **MANY RED CANDIES, LIKE RED M&MS AND RED SKITTLES, GET THEIR VIBRANT COLOR FROM CARMINE, A DYE MADE FROM CRUSHED COCHINEAL BUGS.**

These insects are harvested, dried, and ground up to produce the colorant.

4 **I WILL ASK MY MOM TO MAKE OUR OWN PEANUT BUTTER!**

A typical jar of peanut butter is allowed to contain one or more rodent hairs and an average of 30 or more insect fragments per 100 grams before it is considered unsanitary.

SOME VANILLA FLAVORINGS ARE MADE FROM CASTOREUM, A SUBSTANCE PRODUCED BY BEAVERS AND FOUND IN THEIR CASTOR SACS, WHICH ARE LOCATED NEAR THEIR TAILS.

This beaver butt secretion is used in food and perfumes.

ONE KILOGRAM OF WHEAT CAN CONTAIN UP TO 9 RODENT POOP PELLETS, AND EVEN YOUR FAVORITE POPCORN MAY CONTAIN UP TO 4 PELLETS OF RODENT POOP.

While it sounds gross, small amounts are considered safe for consumption.

THERE'S ALWAYS A TRACE AMOUNT OF COW FECES IN ALL MILK.

The pasteurization process kills harmful bacteria, but the thought might still give you the chills.

CANDY CORN, A POPULAR HALLOWEEN TREAT, CONTAINS CONFECTIONER'S GLAZE, WHICH IS ALSO DERIVED FROM THE LAC BUG.

So, you're munching on bug parts with every sweet bite.

HOT DOGS CAN CONTAIN A MIXTURE OF MEATS AND ADDITIVES, INCLUDING SOME PARTS YOU MIGHT NOT EXPECT.

It's not uncommon for traces of bone, skin, and other animal parts to end up in your frankfurter, making this picnic staple a bit spooky.

Hi there, Brave Reader!

Thank you for diving into this spooky adventure with us!

If you had as much fun reading as we did creating it, we'd love to hear your thoughts.

Reviews help other readers discover the book and let us know what you enjoyed the most. Whether it's a favorite fact, a tricky maze, or just the overall experience, your feedback means the world to us.

So, if you have a moment, please leave a review and share the Halloween fun with others!

Scan this QR Code to leave a review!

To thank you, there are some bonuses waiting for you.

Simply scan this QR Code to unlock them!

88

CHAPTER 6

MONSTER TRIVIA

It's time to put your knowledge to the test with some frightfully fun trivia!

In this chapter, we're serving up a cauldron full of questions that blend the eerie with the educational. From creepy creatures to haunted history, these brain teasers will challenge even the most seasoned spooky scholars.

So, sharpen your wits, gather your courage, and get ready to dive into a world of trivia that's equal parts fun and fear!

1. WHICH COUNTRY IS BELIEVED TO BE THE BIRTHPLACE OF HALLOWEEN?

A.   Ireland

B.   USA

C.   Canada

D.   Mexico

2. WHICH FAMOUS MAGICIAN DIED ON HALLOWEEN?

A.   David Copperfield

B.   Criss Angel

C.   Harry Houdini

D.   David Blaine

3. WHICH FRUIT IS USED FOR A TRADITIONAL HALLOWEEN GAME WHERE PEOPLE TRY TO GRAB THEM WITH THEIR TEETH FROM A WATER-FILLED BASIN?

A.   Oranges

B.   Apples

C.   Grapes

D.   Peaches

1

Answer: A) Ireland.

Cool Fact:

Halloween originated from the ancient Celtic festival of Samhain, celebrated in Ireland. During Samhain, people would light bonfires and wear costumes to ward off ghosts. The tradition spread to other countries and evolved into Halloween we know today.

2

Answer: C) Harry Houdini

Cool Fact:

The legendary escape artist Harry Houdini died on October 31, 1926. Known for his incredible escape acts, Houdini's death on Halloween only added to his mystique and the legends surrounding his life.

3

Answer: B) Apples

Cool Fact:

The game is called bobbing for apples, a fun activity at Halloween parties. It dates back to a Roman festival honoring Pomona, the goddess of fruit and trees, which was merged with the Celtic festival of Samhain when the Romans conquered Britain.

4. IN WHICH CENTURY DID HALLOWEEN FIRST BECOME POPULAR IN AMERICA?

A.   17th century

B.   18th century

C.   19th century

D.   20th century

5. WHAT VEGETABLE WAS ORIGINALLY USED TO MAKE JACK-O'-LANTERNS BEFORE PUMPKINS?

A.   Potatoes

B.   Turnips

C.   Carrots

D.   Squash

6. WHICH ICONIC HALLOWEEN MOVIE FEATURES THREE WITCHES WHO WERE RESURRECTED IN SALEM, MASSACHUSETTS?

A.   The Witches

B.   Hocus Pocus

C.   Practical Magic

D.   The Craft

Answer: C) 19th century

Cool Fact:

Irish and Scottish immigrants brought Halloween traditions to America in the 1800s. The holiday gradually grew in popularity and became widely celebrated by the 20th century.

Answer: B) Turnips

Cool Fact:

The Irish originally carved faces into turnips before discovering pumpkins in America. Pumpkins were larger and easier to carve, making them the perfect choice for creating Jack-o'-lanterns.

Answer: B) Hocus Pocus

Cool Fact:

"Hocus Pocus" is a beloved Halloween movie about the Sanderson sisters returning to Salem. Released in 1993, the film has become a cult classic and is a must-watch for many during Halloween.

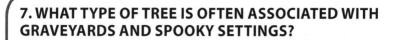

7. WHAT TYPE OF TREE IS OFTEN ASSOCIATED WITH GRAVEYARDS AND SPOOKY SETTINGS?

A.   Oak

B.   Willow

C.   Cypress

D.   Maple

8. WHICH BIRD IS CONSIDERED AN OMEN OF DEATH AND IS OFTEN FEATURED IN HORROR STORIES?

A.   Crow

B.   Sparrow

C.   Robin

D.   Eagle

9. WHAT NATURAL PHENOMENON IS SOMETIMES CALLED "WILL-O'-THE-WISP" AND IS OFTEN SEEN IN MARSHY AREAS?

A.   Aurora Borealis

B.   Bioluminescence

C.   Swamp Gas

D.   St. Elmo's Fire

Answer: C) Cypress

Cool Fact:

Cypress trees are often associated with graveyards and spooky settings. Their dark, dense foliage and twisted branches create an eerie atmosphere, making them a common sight in haunted scenes and cemeteries.

Answer: A) Crow

Cool Fact:

Crows are considered omens of death and are often featured in horror stories. Their black feathers and loud, cawing calls contribute to their spooky reputation, and they are frequently associated with witches and dark magic.

Answer: C) Swamp Gas

Cool Fact:

"Will-o'-the-Wisp" is a natural phenomenon often seen in marshy areas, caused by the combustion of gasses emitted by decaying organic matter. These mysterious lights have inspired many ghost stories and legends about spirits, leading travelers astray.

10. WHAT GHOSTLY NATURAL PHENOMENON OCCURS WHEN A LAYER OF COLD AIR IS TRAPPED BENEATH A LAYER OF WARM AIR, CAUSING STRANGE SOUNDS TO TRAVEL LONG DISTANCES?

A.   Mirage

B.   Fog

C.   Temperature Inversion

D.   Heatwave

11. WHICH MARINE CREATURE GLOWS IN THE DARK DUE TO BIOLUMINESCENCE?

A.   Jellyfish

B.   Shark

C.   Dolphin

D.   Octopus

12. WHICH INSECT IS KNOWN FOR ITS ABILITY TO MIMIC DEAD LEAVES, ADDING TO ITS SPOOKY NATURE?

A.   Praying Mantis

B.   Walking Stick

C.   Leaf Insect

D.   Cicada

10

Answer: C) Temperature Inversion

Cool Fact:

When an inversion layer is present, if a sound or explosion occurs at ground level, the sound waves bend and bounce back to the ground, making them louder or travel faster than usual. This can create eerie, unexplained noises, adding to the spooky atmosphere of certain areas.

11

Answer: A) Jellyfish

Cool Fact:

It is estimated that about 50% of jellyfish are bioluminescent. This eerie glow is produced by chemical reactions within their bodies and has inspired many tales of ghostly sea creatures.

12

Answer: C) Leaf Insect

Cool Fact:

Leaf insects are known for their ability to mimic dead leaves, blending seamlessly into their surroundings. This camouflage helps them avoid predators and adds to their mysterious and spooky allure.

13. WHAT IS THE NAME OF THE GHOSTLY SHIP THAT IS SAID TO SAIL THE SEAS WITH A CREW DOOMED TO SAIL FOREVER?

A.   The Black Pearl

B.   The Flying Dutchman

C.   The Mary Celeste

D.   The Ghost Galleon

14. WHAT IS THE ONLY HUMAN ORGAN THAT CAN REGENERATE ITSELF?

A.   Heart

B.   Liver

C.   Kidney

D.   Lung

15. WHAT PART OF THE HUMAN BODY IS HOME TO THE MOST BACTERIA?

A.   Mouth

B.   Skin

C.   Intestines

D.   Hair

13

Answer: B) The Flying Dutchman

Cool Fact:

The Flying Dutchman is a legendary ghost ship said to sail the seas with a crew doomed to sail forever. The story originated in the 17th century and has become a popular maritime legend, often featured in literature and movies.

14

Answer: B) Liver

Cool Fact:

The liver is the only human organ that can regenerate itself. Even if up to 75% of the liver is removed, it can grow back to its full size, making it a truly remarkable organ.

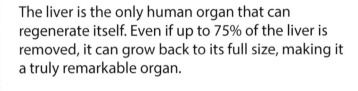

15

Answer: C) Intestines

Cool Fact:

The intestines are home to the most bacteria in the human body. These bacteria, known as gut flora, play a crucial role in digestion and overall health. Still, their sheer number and variety can be surprising.

16. HOW LONG CAN FINGERNAILS CONTINUE TO GROW AFTER DEATH?

A.   A few hours

B.   A few days

C.   A few weeks

D.   They don't grow

17. WHAT PART OF THE HUMAN BODY CONTAINS ABOUT 25% OF THE BONES?

A.   Hands

B.   Feet

C.   Spine

D.   Skull

18. WHAT UNUSUAL SUBSTANCE CAN THE HUMAN STOMACH DISSOLVE?

A.   Metal

B.   Glass

C.   Plastic

D.   Wood

16

Answer: D) They don't grow
Cool Fact:

Fingernails do not actually continue to grow after death. The appearance of growth is due to the skin retracting as the body dehydrates, making the nails and hair seem longer.

17

Answer: B) Feet
Cool Fact:

The feet contain about 25% of the bones in the human body. Each foot has 26 bones, making a total of 52 bones in both feet, which is a significant portion of the 206 bones in the entire body.

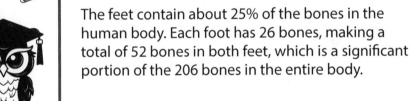

18

Answer: A) Metal
Cool Fact:

The human stomach can dissolve metal, specifically small bits of metal like razor blades. The stomach's highly acidic environment (with a pH of 1.5 to 3.5) is strong enough to break down these materials.

19. WHICH PART OF THE HUMAN BODY IS ENTIRELY UNIQUE TO EACH PERSON, LIKE A FINGERPRINT?

A.   Tongue print

B.   Retina

C.   Ear shape

D.   All of the above

20. WHAT IS THE NAME OF THE FRIENDLY GHOST IN A POPULAR CHILDREN'S CARTOON AND COMIC SERIES?

A.   Casper

B.   Spooky

C.   Boo-Boo

D.   Ghostie

21. WHAT COSTUME IS ONE OF THE MOST POPULAR CHOICES FOR KIDS ON HALLOWEEN?

A.   Superhero

B.   Witch

C.   Ghost

D.   Pirate

19

Answer: D) All of the above
Cool Fact:

All of the above—tongue prints, retinas, and ear shapes—are entirely unique to each person. These unique features can be used for identification, similar to fingerprints.

20

Answer: A) Casper
Cool Fact:

Casper the Friendly Ghost is a popular character who has been charming audiences since the 1940s. Unlike other ghosts, Casper is kind-hearted and always looking to make friends, making him a beloved figure in Halloween culture.

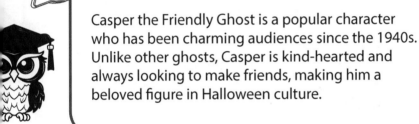

21

Answer: B) Witch
Cool Fact:

The witch is one of the most popular costumes for kids on Halloween. With its pointy hat, broomstick, and cauldron, the witch has become a staple of Halloween attire for both kids and adults.

22. WHAT GAS, MAKING UP 24% OF OUR UNIVERSE, IS RUNNING OUT ON EARTH?

A.   Oxygen

B.   Nitrogen

C.   Helium

D.   Carbon Dioxide

23. TO DATE, WHAT PERCENTAGE OF THE OCEAN HAVE SCIENTISTS BEEN ABLE TO EXPLORE AND ACCOUNT FOR?

A.   50%

B.   25%

C.   10%

D.   Less than 10%

24. WHEN WILL THE NEXT FULL MOON BE ON HALLOWEEN?

A.   2025

B.   2030

C.   2035

D.   2039

22

Answer: C) Helium

Cool Fact:

Helium, which makes up 24% of the elemental mass of the universe, is a non-renewable resource on Earth. It escapes our atmosphere because it is very light, rising until it eventually leaves the planet entirely.

23

Answer: D) Less than 10%

Cool Fact:

Scientists have only been able to explore and account for less than 10% of the ocean. This vast, mysterious frontier holds many secrets and potential discoveries yet to be made.

24

Answer: D) 2039

Cool Fact:

The next full moon to occur on Halloween will be in 2039. Full moons on Halloween are rare, happening only about once every 19 years. This spooky spectacle adds an extra layer of mystery and excitement to the already eerie holiday.

25. WHAT WAS THE ORIGINAL NAME OF CANDY CORN?

A. Sweet Corn

B. Chicken Feed

C. Harvest Treat

D. Autumn Delight

26. WHICH COUNTRY HOLDS THE RECORD FOR THE HEAVIEST PUMPKIN EVER?

A. Italy

B. America

C. Germany

D. Australia

27. HOW MANY COLORS OF M&MS ARE THERE IN A NORMAL BAG?

A. Four

B. Five

C. Six

D. Seven

25

Answer: B) Chicken Feed

Cool Fact:

Candy corn was originally called "Chicken Feed" when it was created in the 1880s. This tri-colored candy was designed to look like corn kernels, which were commonly used as food for chickens, hence the name. Today, it's a staple treat of the Halloween season.

26

Answer: B) America

Cool Fact:

The heaviest pumpkin weighed 2,749 pounds (1,246.9 kilograms) when it was presented by Travis Gienger (USA) at the 50th Safeway World Championship Pumpkin Weigh-Off held in Half Moon Bay, California, USA, on 9 October 2023.

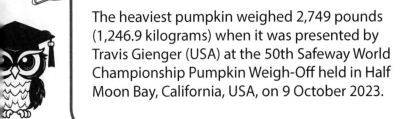

27

Answer: C) Six

Cool Fact:

A regular bag of M&Ms contains six colors: red, orange, yellow, green, blue, and brown. These colorful candies have been a favorite treat since their introduction in 1941, adding a vibrant touch to snacks and desserts.

28. WHAT IS THE MOST POPULAR COSTUME FOR CATS AND DOGS IN THE US?

A.   Witch

B.   Superhero

C.   Pumpkin

D.   Bumblebee

29. WHICH OF THESE URBAN LEGENDS WAS INVENTED BY THE INTERNET?

A.   Bloody Mary

B.   Slender Man

C.   Umm Al Duwais

D.   Chupacabra

30. WHY SHOULD A PERSON WEAR A COSTUME ON HALLOWEEN?

A.   To join in the fun

B.   To receive candy

C.   To deceive evil spirits

D.   To scare friends

28

Answer: C) Pumpkin
Cool Fact:

The most popular costume for cats and dogs is a pumpkin. This adorable and festive outfit is followed by other favorites like hot dog, superhero, and bumblebee, making pets look extra cute during Halloween festivities.

29

Answer: B) Slender Man
Cool Fact:

Slender Man originated as a meme on the website Creepypasta. This eerie figure is depicted as an unusually tall, thin, human-like entity with a featureless face and black suit, haunting forests and abducting children, adding to its internet-born legend.

30

Answer: C) To deceive evil spirits
Cool Fact:

Wearing costumes on Halloween is a tradition that dates back hundreds of years. People believed that by wearing scary costumes, they could trick real ghosts into thinking they were fellow spirits, thus avoiding harm. This ancient practice evolved into the modern custom of dressing up for Halloween.

CHAPTER 7

BOO'S SPOOKTACULAR PARTY

THE SECRET LETTER

Boo is known for his love of games and puzzles, especially when it comes to his Halloween parties.

This year, he's decided to challenge his friends with a special invitation. You've been invited to Boo's Halloween party, but when you open the mail, you find that all the words are scrambled!

FACT

Did you know that your brain can still read scrambled words if the first and last letters are in place?

This happens because your brain reads words as whole units and predicts what it expects to see.

However, this tricky process can slow down your reading by about 11%. It's easier with shorter, more predictable words.

This fascinating ability, sometimes called "Typoglycaemia," shows how powerful your brain is at solving puzzles!

Let's see if you can read Boo's letter! Here's the spooktacular message he sent you.

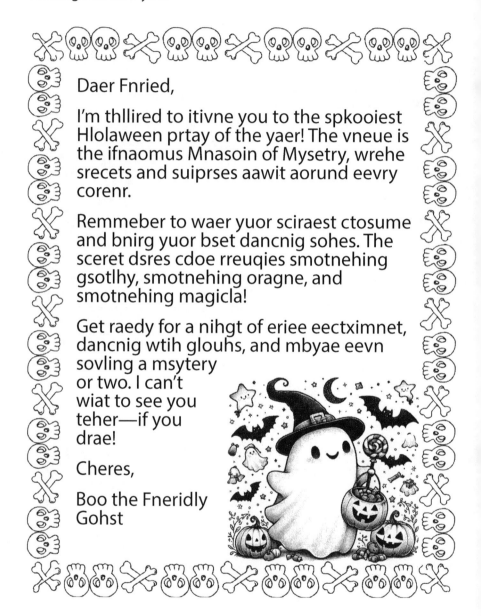

Daer Fnried,

I'm thllired to itivne you to the spkooiest Hlolaween prtay of the yaer! The vneue is the ifnaomus Mnasoin of Mysetry, wrehe srecets and suiprses aawit aorund eevry corenr.

Remmeber to waer yuor sciraest ctosume and bnirg yuor bset dancnig sohes. The sceret dsres cdoe rreuqies smotnehing gsotlhy, smotnehing oragne, and smotnehing magicla!

Get raedy for a nihgt of eriee eectximnet, dancnig wtih glouhs, and mbyae eevn sovling a msytery or two. I can't wiat to see you teher—if you drae!

Cheres,

Boo the Fneridly Gohst

Write down Boo's letter here after you decode it.

MYSTERIOUS COSTUME SHOP

You're on the hunt for the perfect outfit to wear to Boo's spooktacular Halloween party. But there's a twist! Each costume can hold clues to decode a fun puzzle.

Each coded space has two numbers. The first number tells you which costume to look at, and the second number tells you which letter in that costume to use.

For example, if the code is 5-4, you start with the 5th costume, CLOWN. Then, count to the 4th letter, and you'll discover the letter W. Ready to crack the codes and find the right outfit?

COSTUME LIST

1. ASTRONAUT
2. VAMPIRE
3. NINJA
4. PIRATE
5. CLOWN
6. ZOMBIE
7. WEREWOLF
8. KNIGHT
9. DRAGON

What's a pirate's favorite letter?

___ ___ ___ ___ ___ ___ ___
5-2 6-6 8-6 8-6 4-6 9-2 5-1

What's a vampire's favorite holiday?

___ ___ ___ ___ ___ ___ ___ ___ ___
7-8 3-5 8-2 9-4 1-2 9-4 4-2 2-1 8-3 5-5 9-4

Why did the knight bring a pencil to the battle?

___ ___   ___ ___ ___ ___
8-6 9-5   9-1 7-3 1-1 7-1

___   ___ ___ ___ ___ ___
1-1   1-2 7-5 5-3 4-3 9-1

What kind of music do mummies listen to?

___ ___ ___ ___   ___ ___ ___ ___ ___
5-4 9-2 4-4 2-4   6-3 1-8 1-2 8-3 5-1

THE MAD MATH HOUSE

You arrive at Boo's party, and you notice that Boo has a mischievous grin—he claims he can read your mind!

In his house, you will go from room to room as Boo guides you. During the trip, you will find a few numbers to do some math.

As you follow Boo's direction, write down your numbers after each step. Do the math yourself, but don't worry—Boo's got a trick up his sleeve! No matter what numbers you pick, Boo will magically reveal your final number.

Ready, set, Boo!

1. Before you step inside, pick any number you like, write it in the box beside, but don't tell Boo!

2. Creep into the kitchen, find the refrigerator, and add the number on it to your number.

3. Tiptoe up the staircase. Multiply your new number by the number you find on the stairs.

4. Enter the living room, add the number on the haunted couch to your number.

5. Go to the bedroom and subtract the number you find on the blanket from your number.

6. Climb up to the attic. Divide your new number by the number on the wall.

7. Now, find the lamp that is marked with an X. Subtract the number you picked in step 1.

Your final number is 9!

Did Boo just read your mind?

Try again if you dare!

SOLUTION

1. THE SECRET LETTER

Dear Friend,

I'm thrilled to invite you to the spookiest Halloween party of the year! The venue is the infamous Mansion of Mystery, where secrets and surprises await around every corner.

Remember to wear your scariest costume and bring your best dancing shoes. The secret dress code requires something ghostly, something orange, and something magical!

Get ready for a night of eerie excitement, dancing with ghouls, and maybe even solving a mystery or two. I can't wait to see you there—if you dare!

Cheers,
Boo the Friendly Ghost

2. MYSTERIOUS COSTUME SHOP

a. What's a pirate's favorite letter?

Letter C

b. What's a vampire's favorite holiday?

Fangsgiving

c. Why did the knight bring a pencil to the battle?

To draw a sword

d. What kind of music do mummies listen to?

Wrap music

3. THE MAD MATH HOUSE

The math in step 7 cancels out the original number you picked, so no matter which number you choose, the final result will always be the same. This ensures that Boo's spooky trick works every time!

CONCLUSION

As you close the book on this spooky adventure, don't let the curiosity end here! There's a whole world of incredible facts and fun waiting for you.

If you enjoyed this journey, why not keep the fun going?

Check out my other books, *Mind-Blowing Facts For Curious Minds* for over 250 amazing facts from history, nature, science, and beyond—plus, it's loaded with trivia and interactive games like myths vs. facts and a scavenger hunt!

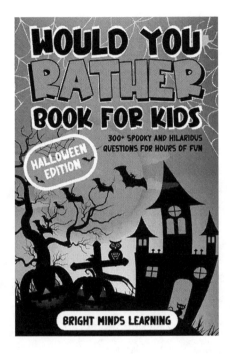

And if you're still in the Halloween spirit, don't miss the *Would You Rather Halloween edition* for more spooky fun and thought-provoking questions.

Keep exploring, keep questioning, and most of all—keep having fun!

Made in United States
Troutdale, OR
09/30/2024

23283706R00069